Dear _____,

How do I say thanks for all that you do? Day after day you're here for me. You greet me each morning with a sunny smile and send me home at the end of each day with lots of great new ideas bubbling in my head. *You make coming to school fun!*

I hope this little book will help to brighten each day of your school year. Because I know that even though I think you're the greatest teacher ever, your job isn't always easy and there are days when you could use a little encouragement— in just the same way you encourage me!

Thank You for Being My Teacher!

_____

Thank You for Being My Teacher!

By
Melody Carlson

HONOR HB BOOKS

FROM DAVID C. COOK

THANK YOU FOR BEING MY TEACHER!
Published by Honor Books®, an imprint of
David C. Cook
4050 Lee Vance View
Colorado Springs, CO 80918 U.S.A.

David C. Cook Distribution Canada
55 Woodslee Avenue, Paris, Ontario, Canada N3L 3E5

David C. Cook U.K., Kingsway Communications
Eastbourne, East Sussex BN23 6NT, England

David C. Cook and the graphic circle C logo
are registered trademarks of Cook Communications Ministries.

The Web site addresses recommended throughout this book are
offered as a resource to you. These Web sites are not intended in any way
to be or imply an endorsement on the part of Cook Communications
Ministries, nor do we vouch for their content.

Unless otherwise noted, Scripture quotations are taken from the *Holy Bible: New International Version*®. NIV®. Copyright © 1973, 1978, 1984 by International Bible Society. Used by permission of Zondervan. All rights reserved. Scripture quotations marked MSG are taken from *THE MESSAGE*. Copyright © by Eugene H. Peterson 1993, 2002. Used by permission of NavPress Publishing Group; NKJV are taken from the New King James Version. Copyright © 1982 by Thomas Nelson, Inc. Used by permission. All rights reserved; and NRSV are taken from the New Revised Standard Version Bible, copyright 1989, Division of Christian Education of the National Council of Christ in the United States of America. Used by permission. All rights reserved.

ISBN 978-0-7814-4546-7

© 2007 Melody Carlson
Published in association with the literary agency of Sara A. Fortenberry.

Cover Design: The DesignWorks Group
Cover Photo: Steve Gardner, PixelWorks Studios

Printed in Canada
First Edition 2007

1 2 3 4 5 6 7 8 9 10

061407

For all those teachers who've made
a difference in my life:
Mrs. Denning, Mrs. Newman, Mr. Batch,
Mr. Lamb, Mr. Hanley, Mrs. Hagebush,
Mrs. Morin, Mr. Mortenson, Mrs. Young …
and those thousands of others
who touch the hearts and minds
of young people daily.

I Thank You!

A good teacher remembers what it was like

to be taught by their favorite teacher.

— Robert McLain

Contents

Autumn Dreams

N n   O o   P p   Q q   R r   S s   T t   U u   V v   W w   X x   Y y   Z z

Autumn Dreams cont.

Winter Works

A a   B b   C c   D d   E e   F f   G g   H h   I i   J j   K k   L l   M m

Winter Works cont.

N n   O o   P p   Q q   R r   S s   T t   U u   V v   W w   X x   Y y   Z z

Winter Works cont.

Spring Blossoms

Aa Bb Cc Dd Ee Ff Gg Hh Ii Jj Kk Ll Mm

Spring Blossoms cont.

Nn Oo Pp Qq Rr Ss Tt Uu Vv Ww Xx Yy Zz

Cc Dd Ee Ff Gg Hh Ii Jj Kk Ll Mm Nn Oo Pp Qq Rr Ss Tt Uu Vv Ww Xx Yy

Autumn Dreams

A time of gathering back together
Eager minds, young hearts, fresh voices
Warm and slightly weary from summer
Yet full of unexpressed hopes and dreams
And bright expectations of what lies ahead
School is back in session!

YOU ARE A TEACHER!

Have you ever had one of those end-of-summer, before-school-starts nightmares in which buckets of purple paint spill from the ceiling and three-headed "children" speak to you in foreign tongues? But suddenly you wake up and remember that you are a teacher and school is about to start! Although there may be challenges in the classroom, thankfully, they will be nothing like your before-school-starts nightmare. And because *you are a teacher,* you're up for the challenge.

But as the first day of school grows closer, a sense of hope and anticipation begins to sweep over you. You wonder how many children will be in your class this year. Will there be a couple of geniuses amid the bunch? A class clown? A child with wide eyes who's too shy to speak? You think about the children who will soon become your new little friends, who will look up to you with love and admiration … and with great expectation—simply because *you are a teacher!*

Aa Bb Cc Dd Ee Ff Gg Hh Ii Jj Kk Ll Mm

It's a time of hopeful wonder, mixed with the realization that there will also be trials and struggles ahead. Perhaps you'll encounter a parent who's difficult, a child who's suffered abuse, or one with behavioral problems. You know what to expect because it's all just part of the teaching life.

And yet you look forward to it, because *you are a teacher!* You are ready to take on these challenges and transform them into bright successes. You have a sharp mind and a caring heart—not to mention a witty sense of humor. For *you are a teacher!*

You appreciate the value of the young lives that have been entrusted to you. And you realize the investment you are making in the future. You don't take these responsibilities lightly, yet you know how to laugh and have fun. When the going gets tough, you know how to pray.

FOR YOU ARE A TEACHER!

BEGINNINGS

The beginning is the most
important part of the work.

—Plato

All glory comes from daring to begin.

—Eugene F. Ware

A journey of a thousand miles must
begin with a single step.

—Lao Tzu

He who chooses the beginning of a road chooses
the place it leads to. It is
the means that determine the end.

—Harry Emerson Fosdick

Aa Bb Cc Dd Ee Ff Gg Hh Ii Jj Kk Ll Mm

THE TIME HAS COME

Anticipation building,

The bulletin board is up,

The pungent smell of clean and shining floors,

Desks squared off into neat rows—

A new school year about to begin!

Hopes, desires, expectations …

Young minds, like sponges, eager to learn,

Thirsting for knowledge

(whether they know it or not).

A silent prayer upon my heart:

Teach me to teach—again.

AN APPLE A DAY

(Recipe for an Excellent Teacher)

A is for aptitude—intelligence to teach.

P is for patience—when they're hard to reach.

P is for prayer—when my day's work is done.

L is for love—may I love *everyone!*

E is for empathy—a feeling heart.

Mix them together, and now we start!

A a B b C c D d E e F f G g H h I i J j K k L l M m

FRESH STARTS

Knowledge rests on knowledge;
what is new is meaningful because it departs
slightly from what was known before.

—Robert Oppenheimer

Teaching is a rigorous act of faith.

—Susan Ohanian

Once children learn how to learn,
nothing is going to narrow their minds.
The essence of teaching is to make learning
contagious, to have one idea spark another.

—Marva Collins

Pretty much all the honest truth-telling
there is in the world is done by children.

—Oliver Wendell Holmes

Nn Oo Pp Qq Rr Ss Tt Uu Vv Ww Xx Yy Zz

WHY GOD CREATED
TEACHERS

When God created teachers,

He gave us special friends

To help us understand His world

And truly comprehend

The beauty and the wonder

Of everything we see,

And become a better person

With each discovery.

When God created teachers,

He gave us special guides

To show us ways in which to grow

So we can all decide

How to live and how to do

What's right instead of wrong,

To lead us so that we can lead

And learn how to be strong.

A a B b C c D d E e F f G g H h I i J j K k L l M m

Why God created teachers,

In His wisdom and His grace,

Was to help us learn to make our world

A better, wiser place.

—Kevin William Huff

FIRST-IMPRESSION PRAYER

May I smile at each new student
And remember each new name.
May I make each child feel special
And know they're not the same.

May my words be kind and patient
And the best that they can be.
Please help my first impression
To reflect the love in me.

Amen.

TIMELESS TIDBITS
OF WISDOM

You cannot teach a man anything;
you can only help him find it within himself.

—Galileo

I have never let my schooling
interfere with my education.

—Mark Twain

It is the supreme art of the teacher to awaken joy
in creative expression and knowledge.

—Albert Einstein

OUR FINEST EXAMPLE

You address me as "Teacher" and "Master,"

and rightly so. That is what I am.

So if I, the Master and Teacher, washed your feet,

you must now wash each other's feet.

I've laid down a pattern for you.

What I've done, you do.

—Jesus Christ, John 13:13–15 MSG

Aa Bb Cc Dd Ee Ff Gg Hh Ii Jj Kk Ll Mm

TEACHER'S BLESSING

May my class size be manageable,

And my recess duties light.

May my parents be supportive,

And my principal kind and understanding.

And if all else fails,

May I grow in wisdom and patience each day,

And may summer come quickly!

BLANK SLATES

Education's purpose is to replace
an empty mind with an open one.

—Malcolm S. Forbes

The teacher who is indeed wise does not
bid you to enter the house of his wisdom
but rather leads you to the threshold of your mind.

—Kahlil Gibran

Every child is an artist. The problem is how to
remain an artist once he grows up.

—Pablo Picasso

Aa Bb Cc Dd Ee Ff Gg Hh Ii Jj Kk Ll Mm

SEEING DEEPER

Oh, that I might realize

What it is that makes each child tick.

May I not see by sight alone,

Or pass a judgment—too quick.

May I listen, watch, and wait,

View them through their Maker's eyes,

So my teaching reaches deeper,

As I learn to be more wise.

Nn Oo Pp Qq Rr Ss Tt Uu Vv Ww Xx Yy Zz

THE MIRACLE OF THE
BEGINNING READER

I wriggle and I jiggle,

And I rock upon my chair.

I wiggle a loose tooth,

And I twirl a strand of hair.

I chew on several fingers,

And I sometimes suck my thumb.

I tap the reading table

Like I'd play upon a drum.

I kick my foot with rhythm,

And lose the place where I should look.

I rub my nose and clear my throat,

And sometimes drop my book.

I look outside the window,

And I look down at the floor.

I pay very close attention

When someone's at the door.

I close my eyes and rest my head;

My teacher's heart must bleed.

But in spite of all of this,

I'm learning how to read!

—Jane Miller

N n O o P p Q q R r S s T t U u V v W w X x Y y Z z

CREATIVITY

The whole art of teaching is only the art of
awakening the natural curiosity of young minds for
the purpose of satisfying it afterwards.

—Anatole France

One must learn by doing the thing;
for though you think you know it,
you have no certainty until you try.

—Sophocles

The best way to know life is to love many things.

—Vincent van Gogh

An artist is always out of step with the time.
He has to be.

—Orson Welles

Wonder is the desire for knowledge.

—St. Thomas Aquinas

Aa Bb Cc Dd Ee Ff Gg Hh Ii Jj Kk Ll Mm

TWICE AND AGAIN

Most will agree that the ability to teach really well is a rare gift indeed. Certainly, not just anyone can stand up before a crowded classroom and impart understandable knowledge to a bunch of squirming kids. It requires practice, perseverance, and patience to present meaningful lessons—day after day, year after year. And it takes intelligence, substance, and skill to make education practical and memorable for students. And then there are always those challenging moments when teachers must call upon the deepest resources—qualities like humor, honesty, mercy, and love.

But the sad truth is, not all teachers are prepared for this demanding task of changing young lives—and yet, what a rare blessing when they are! For as teachers rise to the occasion, they bestow a priceless gift upon their students. In fact, they're investing in the future for us all!

So then, what is the secret of truly great teachers?

What is that hidden edge that some teachers seem to naturally possess?

How is it that some teachers are able to inspire children to learn, igniting their hunger for knowledge? How did they

Nn Oo Pp Qq Rr Ss Tt Uu Vv Ww Xx Yy Zz

become so adept and intuitive in their ability to spark a child's interest?

Perhaps it's because they, as teachers, have never stopped being students themselves. Perhaps it's a deep love for learning that guides them. It could also be their committed respect for knowledge and the understanding that they themselves will never fully arrive, never know it all. Maybe it's that hunger within their hearts for learning that reveals to them new and exciting ways to teach.

If these things are true, great teachers are doubly blessed: not only do they experience the thrill of successful teaching, but they also receive the satisfaction of continuing their own academic journey as well.

1 + 1 = 2

To teach is to learn twice.

—Joseph Joubert

To know how to suggest is the great art of teaching.

—Henri Frédéric Amiel

The moment you stop learning, you stop leading.

—Rick Warren

Acquire new knowledge whilst thinking over the old,
and you may become a teacher of others.

—Confucius

Nn Oo Pp Qq Rr Ss Tt Uu Vv Ww Xx Yy Zz

AN APPLE

An apple lasts a short time
In the hands of a teacher.
A bit of wisdom lasts a lifetime
In the mind of a child.

—Unknown

LET THEM COME

Let the little children come to Me, and do not forbid them;
for of such is the kingdom of God. Assuredly, I say to you,
whoever does not receive the kingdom of God as a little
child will by no means enter it.

—Jesus Christ, Luke 18:16–17 NKJV

A WORD FROM THE WISE

The human mind is not capable of grasping the Universe. We are like a little child entering a huge library. The walls are covered to the ceiling with books in many different tongues. The child knows that someone must have written these books. It does not know who or how. It does not understand the languages in which they are written. But the child notes a definite plan in the arrangement of the books, a mysterious order it does not comprehend, but only dimly suspects.

—Albert Einstein

Aa Bb Cc Dd Ee Ff Gg Hh Ii Jj Kk Ll Mm

CLASSROOM RIDDLES

What is warm and fuzzy and has four arms?

A hug!

What is only inches long but contains a mile?

A smile!

What is highly contagious but incredibly healthy?

Laughter!

What is inexpensive to give but priceless to receive?

Love!

Nn Oo Pp Qq Rr Ss Tt Uu Vv Ww Xx Yy Zz

I SHALL NOT PASS THIS WAY AGAIN

Through this toilsome world, alas!

Once and only once I pass;

If a kindness I may show,

If a good deed I may do

To a suffering fellow man,

Let me do it while I can.

No delay, for it is plain

I shall not pass this way again.

—Unknown

PREPARING FOR
THE FUTURE

It is better to build children than to repair adults.

—Unknown

If the children are untaught, their ignorance and
vices will in future life cost us much dearer in their
consequences than it would have done in their
correction by a good education.

—Thomas Jefferson

Human history becomes more and more a race
between education and catastrophe.

—H. G. Wells

Nn Oo Pp Qq Rr Ss Tt Uu Vv Ww Xx Yy Zz

DIVINE GUIDANCE

Trust in the LORD with all your heart,

and lean not on your own understanding;

in all your ways acknowledge Him,

and He shall direct your paths.

—Proverbs 3:5–6 NKJV

I will instruct you and teach you

in the way you should go;

I will counsel you and watch over you.

—Psalm 32:8

Aa Bb Cc Dd Ee Ff Gg Hh Ii Jj Kk Ll Mm

GATHER THE LEAVES!

What is it about autumn leaves—those glorious shades of orange, red, gold, and russet—that fill the heart with such pure joy? Take a group of grade-school children on a field trip through a leaf-strewn park and you will see that it's purely instinctual to run through the colorful carpet of leaves, to kick them high or throw them into the air, or even get down and roll in them like a dog. And if you were to give children rakes, chances are they would gather the leaves into bright mounds—like pirates' treasure. Oh, sure, they would probably run and jump into them afterward, splaying them all about, but it would be a leap of pure joy.

Is it the crisp autumnal air, the rich changing colors, the shortening of days that fills the soul with such boundless energy? Or is it something more? One can grow philosophical or long-winded as to the impact of autumn on the human heart, but if you are a teacher, you can simply embrace autumn as the time of year when children, as abundant and as colorful as the autumn leaves, are ready to be gathered up and enjoyed by you!

A TEACHER'S SURVIVAL KIT

(found in most teachers' desks)

A Toothpick:

A reminder to point out the good qualities in each of my students.

A Rubber Band:

A reminder to be flexible; things don't always go as planned.

A Bandage:

A reminder that some kids have wounds and may need my help to heal.

A Pencil:

A reminder to list my daily blessings and remind my students to do the same.

A a B b C c D d E e F f G g H h I i J j K k L l M m

An Eraser:

A reminder that I am human and need to forgive and forget mistakes.

A Stick of Gum:

A reminder to "stick" with it and encourage my students to do likewise.

A Mint:

A reminder that my students are worth a mint to me (even if I don't get paid one!).

A Candy Kiss:

A reminder that everyone needs lots of love and hugs and warm squeezes.

A Tea Bag:

A reminder to take time to relax, unwind, refresh, and refuel.

—Unknown

Nn Oo Pp Qq Rr Ss Tt Uu Vv Ww Xx Yy Zz

TRICK OR TREAT

Time to put the books away,
Kids can learn while they're at play.
Time to laugh and joke and share,
How to help and how to care.

Time for pumpkins and black cats,
Spiderwebs and spooky bats.
Time for children in costume,
There's a party in the room!

Time to enjoy what is sweet,
A funny trick or yummy treat.
Time to pause and time to start …
Remember to be young at heart.

NATURAL TEACHERS

Come forth into the light of things,

Let Nature be your teacher.

—William Wordsworth

Awaken people's curiosity. It is enough

to open minds, do not overload them.

Put there just a spark.

—Anatole France

To see a World in a grain of sand

And a Heaven in a wild flower,

Hold Infinity in the palm of your hand,

And Eternity in an hour.

—William Blake

To think creatively, we must be able to look afresh

at what we normally take for granted.

—George Kneller

Nn Oo Pp Qq Rr Ss Tt Uu Vv Ww Xx Yy Zz

TEACHER'S
SERENITY PRAYER

God grant me wisdom, creativity, and love.

With wisdom,

I may look to the future and see the effect

That my teaching will have on these children,

And thus adapt my methods

To fit the needs of each one.

With creativity,

I can prepare new and interesting projects

That challenge my students

And expand their minds

To set higher goals and dream loftier dreams.

Aa Bb Cc Dd Ee Ff Gg Hh Ii Jj Kk Ll Mm

With love,

I can praise my students for jobs well done

And encourage them to get up

And go on when they fail.

Lord, reveal Yourself through me.

Amen.

—Unknown

BOUNDLESSNESS

Our greatest natural resource is
the minds of our children.

—Walt Disney

Children are the living messages we send
to a time we will not see.

—Neil Postman

He who would learn to fly one day
must first learn to stand and walk and run and
climb and dance; one cannot fly into flying.

—Friedrich Nietzsche

Aa Bb Cc Dd Ee Ff Gg Hh Ii Jj Kk Ll Mm

GIVING THANKS

Thank you, Lord,
For making it to here,
Almost three months
Through the school year.

Thank you, Lord,
For each eager heart,
Learning and growing,
And getting so smart.

Thank you, Lord,
For each happy face,
For the cheerful voices
That fill this space.

Bless them, Lord,
As they go their way,
To family and friends
On Thanksgiving Day!

Nn Oo Pp Qq Rr Ss Tt Uu Vv Ww Xx Yy Zz

Cc Dd Ee Ff Gg Hh Ii Jj Kk Ll Mm Nn Oo Pp Qq Rr Ss Tt Uu Vv Ww Xx Yy

Winter Works

A quiet busyness fills the classroom
Little heads bowed low
Engrossed in active learning
Working hard
With eyes, hands, fingers, tongue
All focused on the task
As they are busily becoming
What it is they'll someday be.

MINCING WORDS
OR MINCING PIES?

So what do we call this season now? Do we refer to that special time in December as "the holidays" or "winter" or "Christmas"? Do we have *winter* concerts and sing *winter* carols? Or do we fight to keep the word *Christmas* on the program? Certainly, it's irritating when old traditions are whittled away. Naturally, we want to stand up for what we believe. But there are many ways to remain faithful to our beliefs ... many ways to celebrate what we hold dear.

As teachers, how do we react when battle lines are drawn and voices are raised in anger? Do we take sides, shake our fists, and demand our own way? Or do we pause to remember the real reason for the season? Do we recall that Jesus Christ was born in total humility? Do we remember that He never fought for recognition—political or otherwise? Do we believe that Christ willingly laid down His life as an act of love? Do we try to do the same?

Children learn just as much by observing what we do as they do by hearing what we say. If we follow Jesus' example, if we allow His light to shine through us, won't they learn the true spirit of Christmas—no matter what it is called?

A a   B b   C c   D d   E e   F f   G g   H h   I i   J j   K k   L l   M m

I put the relation of a fine teacher to a student just
below the relation of a mother to a son.

—Thomas Wolfe

You can pay people to teach,
but you can't pay them to care.

—Marva Collins

CHILDREN LEARN
WHAT THEY LIVE

If a child lives with criticism, he learns to condemn.

If a child lives with hostility, he learns to fight.

If a child lives with ridicule, he learns to be shy.

If a child lives with shame, he learns to feel guilty.

If a child lives with tolerance, he learns to be patient.

If a child lives with encouragement, he learns confidence.

If a child lives with praise, he learns to appreciate.

If a child lives with fairness, he learns justice.

If a child lives with security, he learns to have faith.

If a child lives with approval, he learns to like himself.

If a child lives with acceptance, and friendship, he learns to
find love in the world.

—Dorothy Law Nolte, PhD

Aa Bb Cc Dd Ee Ff Gg Hh Ii Jj Kk Ll Mm

A TRULY HONORABLE PROFESSION

As children, we usually either disdained them or looked up to them with awe and respect. Whether we drew derogatory stick-man pictures of them behind their backs or silently admired them from afar, it was impossible not to be affected and impacted by those who taught us. And if, as it turned out, we chose to join them in this strange and often maligned profession (this mysterious field of education), we probably knew that it wouldn't be easy—nor were we in it "for the money."

And yet, we need to remember that it truly is an honorable profession—perhaps not on Wall Street or in the Fortune 500, but over the long haul, when the things that really matter are all added up and accounted for … maybe by then everyone will realize that all good teachers are truly worth their weight in gold. But in the meantime, we might struggle with things like identity, job-related stress, self-worth, and personal validation. But this struggle is only temporary.

For the time will surely come when all values of heaven and earth will be turned upside down, and the things that really mattered all along will be made perfectly plain and

Nn Oo Pp Qq Rr Ss Tt Uu Vv Ww Xx Yy Zz

clear. Things like the nurturing and educating of young minds. Things like love and grace and forgiveness … a helping hand along life's way. And those godly teachers who poured out their hearts and souls into caring for and serving children will be honored. For you see, teaching truly is an honorable profession.

CIRCLE OF LEARNING

We shall not cease from exploration

And the end of all our exploring

Will be to arrive where we started

And know the place for the first time.

—T. S. Eliot

TEACHER'S TREASURE

Do not lay up for yourselves treasures on earth, where moth and rust destroy and where thieves break in and steal; but lay up for yourselves treasures in heaven, where neither moth nor rust destroys and where thieves do not break in and steal. For where your treasure is, there your heart will be also.

—Jesus Christ, Matthew 6:19–21 NKJV

LASTING IMPRESSIONS

Education … is a painful, continual and
difficult work to be done in kindness,
by watching, by warning, … by praise,
but above all—by example.

—John Ruskin

Children are like wet cement.
Whatever falls on them makes an impression.

—Haim Ginott

When teaching, light a fire, don't fill a bucket.

—Dan Snow

Nn Oo Pp Qq Rr Ss Tt Uu Vv Ww Xx Yy Zz

THE MIRACLE OF LEARNING

Like a seed planted some time ago,

Lying in the cold winter ground,

Nearly forgotten,

So many lessons rest, dormant, waiting.

But then, something happens.

A ray of warmth, a sprinkling of understanding,

And, lo, the seed begins to awaken,

Stretching out tender roots, exploring.

Then with a burst of revelation,

The tender bud shoots forth,

Lifting up its face victorious

Toward the light.

And the miracle of learning has begun.

A a   B b   C c   D d   E e   F f   G g   H h   I i   J j   K k   L l   M m

TEACHER'S PRAYER

I want to teach my students how
To live this life on earth,
To face its struggles and its strife
And to improve their worth.

Not just the lesson in a book
Or how the rivers flow,
But how to choose the proper path
Wherever they may go.

To understand eternal truth
And know right from wrong,
And gather all the beauty of
A flower and a song.

For if I help the world to grow
In wisdom and in grace,

Nn Oo Pp Qq Rr Ss Tt Uu Vv Ww Xx Yy Zz

Then I shall feel that I have won
And I have filled my place.

And so I ask your guidance, God,
That I may do my part.
For character and confidence
And happiness of heart.

—James J. Metcalf

THE PRACTICE OF PATIENCE

You can learn many things from children.
How much patience you have, for instance.

—Franklin P. Jones

Blessed are the hearts that can bend;
they shall never be broken.

—Albert Camus

We could never learn to be brave and patient
if there were only joy in the world.

—Helen Keller

One moment of patience may ward off great disaster.
One moment of impatience may ruin a whole life.

—Chinese Proverb

Nn   Oo   Pp   Qq   Rr   Ss   Tt   Uu   Vv   Ww   Xx   Yy   Zz

HOW DO YOU SPELL
PATIENCE?

P *ower* to exercise self-control

A *llow* some things to roll off

T *ime* to take a break

I *nterest* to be given

E *nergy* to think

N *ever* make a stink

C *are* for a young friend

E *ven* this day will end!

A a   B b   C c   D d   E e   F f   G g   H h   I i   J j   K k   L l   M m

WHOSE CHILD IS THIS?

"Whose child is this?" I asked one day,

Seeing a little one out at play.

"Mine," said the parent with tender smile.

"Mine to keep a little while

To bathe his hands and comb his hair

To tell him what he is to wear

To prepare him that he may always be good

And each day do the things he should."

"Whose child is this?" I asked again

As the door opened and someone came in.

"Mine," said the teacher with the same tender smile.

"Mine, to keep for a little while.

To teach him how to be gentle and kind

To train and direct his dear little mind

To help him live by every rule

And get the best he can from school."

In Oo Pp Qq Rr Ss Tt Uu Vv Ww Xx Yy Zz

"Whose child is this?" I asked once more,

Just as the little one entered the door.

"Ours," said the parent and the teacher as they smiled

And each took a hand of the little child.

"Ours, to love and train together,

Ours, this blessed task, forever."

—Unknown

STEP BY STEP

Character cannot be developed in ease and quiet.
Only through experience of trial and suffering
can the soul be strengthened, ambition inspired,
and success achieved.

—Helen Keller

A child educated only at school
is an uneducated child.

—George Santayana

If the only tool you have is a hammer,
you tend to see every problem as a nail.

—Abraham Maslow

PRAYER FOR WISDOM

Dear Lord, as I begin this day,

Make me wise, oh Lord, I pray.

Show me ways to understand

The children placed within my hand.

Lord, I need Your help to learn

How to teach and to discern

What is good and right and true.

Sometimes I don't have a clue.

Dear Lord, I need Your help to see

The needs of those all around me.

I need Your wisdom, Lord, to teach—

To touch a mind, a heart to reach.

Amen.

Aa Bb Cc Dd Ee Ff Gg Hh Ii Jj Kk Ll Mm

LASTING INFLUENCE

The philosophy of the schoolroom in one generation
will be the philosophy of government in the next.

—Abraham Lincoln

The best teacher is the one who suggests
rather than dogmatizes, and inspires his listener
with the wish to teach himself.

—Edward Bulwer-Lytton

What nobler employment, or more valuable
to the state, than that of the man
who instructs the rising generation?

—Marcus Tullius Cicero

Nn Oo Pp Qq Rr Ss Tt Uu Vv Ww Xx Yy Zz

CAN YOU SEE ME?

I'm in your class, well, most of the time anyway.

Sometimes I don't make it (cuz, well, stuff happens).

But sometimes, in your class, I'm invisible.

No one—not you, not the kids—can see me.

And sometimes I imagine I'm superpowered and I can fly

Far, far away from here,

From everything and everyone that hurts me.

But I can't, not really. I can't fly.

Maybe it's because I'm too stupid

Or too slow or too dumb.

That's what some people say,

And maybe they're right.

I don't know for sure.

But can you see me?

A a   B b   C c   D d   E e   F f   G g   H h   I i   J j   K k   L l   M m

TRANSFORMED
TEACHERS

And do not be conformed to this world,

but be transformed by the renewing of your mind,

that you may prove what is that good and

acceptable and perfect will of God.

—Romans 12:2 NKJV

PEOPLE-MAKING

In the final analysis it is not what you do for
your children but what you have taught them to do
for themselves that will make them
successful human beings.

—Ann Landers

He who opens a school door, closes a prison.

—Victor Hugo

A teacher who is attempting to teach
without inspiring the pupil with a desire to learn
is hammering on cold iron.

—Horace Mann

KIDS WHO ARE DIFFERENT

Here's to the kids who are different,

The kids who don't always get A's

The kids who have ears twice the size of their peers,

And noses that go on for days …

Here's to the kids who are different,

The kids they call crazy or dumb.

The kids who don't fit, with the guts or the grit,

Who dance to a different drum …

Here's to the kids who are different,

The kids with the mischievous streak,

For when they have grown, as history's shown,

It's their difference that makes them unique.

Here's to the kids who are different.

—Digby Wolfe

N n   O o   P p   Q q   R r   S s   T t   U u   V v   W w   X x   Y y   Z z

LEARNING NEVER ENDS

Anyone who stops learning is old, whether at twenty
or eighty. Anyone who keeps learning stays young.

—Henry Ford

I cannot teach you; only help you to
explore yourself. Nothing more.

—Bruce Lee

It's not who you are that holds you back,
it's who you think you're not.

—Unknown

You teach best what you most need to learn.

—Richard Bach

Give instruction to the wise, and they will
become wiser still; teach the righteous
and they will gain in learning.

—Proverbs 9:9 NRSV

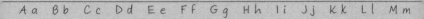

Aa Bb Cc Dd Ee Ff Gg Hh Ii Jj Kk Ll Mm

TEACHING UNIQUENESS

Each second we live is a new and unique moment of the universe, a moment that will never be again. And what do we teach our children? We teach them that two and two makes four, and that Paris is the capital of France. When will we also teach them what they are?

We should say to each of them: Do you know what you are? You are a marvel. You are unique. In all the years that have passed, there has never been another child like you. Your legs, your arms, your clever fingers, the way you move. You may become a Shakespeare, a Michelangelo, a Beethoven. You have the capacity for anything. Yes, you are a marvel.

—Pablo Casals

ODE TO A MUCH-LOVED TEACHER

Just as I was ready to give up

On ever learning anything at all,

I landed in a caring teacher's class—

A man who seemed to clearly know his call.

This teacher understood a line of prose,

Had passion for a fine, well-written book.

At home with Robert Frost and Jack London,

He made his students take a second look.

And so instead of simply giving up,

I found myself enticed to want to learn—

To read, to write, to study all I could;

The hunger in me soon began to burn.

I quickly found that there was much to know!

My teacher couldn't dish it out too fast!

But perhaps the best thing that he taught

Was learning, once begun, will always last.

LEARNING INGREDIENTS

I cannot teach anybody anything;
I can only make them think.

—Socrates

He who dares to teach must never cease to learn.

—Richard Henry Dann

I have learned silence from the talkative, tolerance
from the intolerant, and kindness from the unkind;
yet, strangely, I am ungrateful to these teachers.

—Kahlil Gibran

TREMENDOUS POWER

I've come to the frightening conclusion that I am the decisive element in the classroom. It's my personal approach that creates the climate. It's my daily mood that makes the weather. As a teacher, I possess a tremendous power to make a child's life miserable or joyous. I can be a tool of torture or an instrument of inspiration. I can humiliate or humor, hurt or heal. In all situations, it is my response that decides whether a crisis will be escalated or de-escalated and a child humanized or de-humanized.

—Haim Ginott

WHAT YOU DON'T
KNOW COULD
BLESS YOU

Every single day is a new opportunity to touch the life of a child in a meaningful and memorable way. Yet, so often, teachers, pressed by schedules and recess duty and aptitude tests and interruptions, often lose sight of such significant moments. As they strive to do the tasks before them, care for the needs of their students, and impart a little learning, it's possible they don't even notice the impact they are making.

But little eyes are watching. Young hearts are being affected on a regular basis. And the teachers who are diligently going about the work of teaching are probably touching lives in a multitude of ways that they may never even be aware of. Yet it happens—every school year and possibly every day.

The proof that it happens is tucked safely in all the stories that veteran schoolteachers happen to hear (years after the fact, of course). It happens when Mrs. Johnson meets thirty-three-year-old Jenny White in the grocery store, and Jenny gushes, "You'll never know how much it meant to me that time you sent a note home to my stepmom, telling her how helpful I'd been."

Or when Mr. Davis runs into Jason Oleander (the boy he felt would surely end up in prison), who now looks crisp and neat in his three-piece suit. "Mr. Davis, have I ever thanked you for the way you encouraged me in arithmetic? I'm a CPA now, and I always give all the credit to my fifth-grade math teacher."

Consider all the stories teachers never hear. For each story shared, there must be millions that go untold; however, the impact on society and the gratitude of many remain just the same. Teachers can be sure there are many, many success stories they will never hear or know. But gratitude isn't the reason they're teaching, is it?

SNIPPETS OF SMARTS

The object of teaching a child is to
enable him to get along without his teacher.

—Elbert Hubbard

It is not the answer that enlightens, but the question.

—Eugène Ionesco

Our talents are the gift that God gives to us…. What
we make of our talents is our gift back to God.

—Leo Buscaglia

Knowledge is of two kinds.
We know a subject ourselves, or we know
where we can find information upon it.

—Samuel Johnson

Aa Bb Cc Dd Ee Ff Gg Hh Ii Jj Kk Ll Mm

TEACHER'S PRAYER

Lord, please help me,

To strengthen their voices,

Bodies and minds,

To express their feelings and

Control them sometimes,

To explore what's near

And venture afar,

But most important to love

Who they are.

—Unknown

SUCCESSFUL TEACHING

To waken interest and kindle enthusiasm is
the sure way to teach easily and successfully.

—Tyron Edwards

I hear and I forget. I see and I remember.
I do and I understand.

—Chinese Proverb

The job of an educator is to teach students
to see the vitality in themselves.

—Joseph Campbell

A a   B b   C c   D d   E e   F f   G g   H h   I i   J j   K k   L l   M m

YOU'RE SOMEONE
SPECIAL

Someone special is someone

Who thinks of those in need

And brings a bit of sunshine

With every caring word and deed.

Someone special is someone

Whose sharing makes them part

Of all the treasured memories

That are precious to the heart.

Someone special is someone

Who spreads happiness wherever they go,

A special blessing to the world

And a special joy to know.

—Unknown

Nn Oo Pp Qq Rr Ss Tt Uu Vv Ww Xx Yy Zz

WORDS TO TEACH BY

Everything should be made as simple
as possible, but not simpler.

—Albert Einstein

Courage is what it takes to stand up and speak;
courage is also what it takes to sit down and listen.

—Sir Winston Churchill

Creative activity could be described as a type of
learning process where teacher and pupil
are located in the same individual.

—Arthur Koestler

Challenges are what make life interesting;
overcoming them is what makes life meaningful.

—Joshua J. Marine

Aa Bb Cc Dd Ee Ff Gg Hh Ii Jj Kk Ll Mm

TOUCHED BY A TEACHER

We think of the effective teachers we have had
over the years with a sense of recognition,
but those who have touched our humanity we
remember with a deep sense of gratitude.

—Anonymous Student

I hear, and I forget.

I see, and I remember.

I do, and I understand.

—Confucius

A STUDENT'S PRAISE

Teachers are full of patience.

Teachers never give up

And won't let you give up either.

Teachers take students seriously.

Teachers care in their sleep.

Teachers see the genius

In every drawing, poem, and essay.

Teachers make you feel important.

Teachers also help others.

Teachers never grow old.

Teachers stay famous in their students' minds

Forever.

—Unknown Student Author

Aa Bb Cc Dd Ee Ff Gg Hh Ii Jj Kk Ll Mm

WHAT STUDENTS NEED

Students do not need to be labeled or measured by more than they are. They don't need more federal funds, grants, and gimmicks. What they need from us is common sense, dedication, and bright, energetic teachers who believe that all children are achievers and who take personally the failure of any one child.

—Marva Collins

A teacher who can arouse a feeling for one single good action, for one single good poem, accomplishes more than he who fills our memory with rows on rows of natural objects, classified with name and form.

—Johann Wolfgang von Goethe

Nn Oo Pp Qq Rr Ss Tt Uu Vv Ww Xx Yy Zz

A MORNING BLESSING

May God bless you this day
As you rush on your way
Embracing this life that you live.

May your spirits be bright
And you burdens be light
May your heart be preparing to give.

May discernment abound
And all wisdom be found
With common sense along the way.

May a smile light your face
And your speech be with grace
As you bless those you teach on this day.

—Unknown

Nothing you do for children is ever wasted.

They seem not to notice us, hovering,

averting our eyes, and they seldom offer thanks,

but what we do for them is never wasted.

—Garrison Keillor

A GOOD TOOLBOX

Love: the glue that holds everything together

Joy: the box of brilliant crayons that color our world
with wonder

Peace: the ruler to measure our lives by

Patience: the pencil that can always be resharpened

Gentleness: the soft tissues that wipe away tears

Kindness: the eraser that removes mistakes

Self-Control: the scissors that cut away harsh edges

Endurance: the tennis shoes that are ready to run
and run

GIFTED TEACHERS

But what happens when we live God's way? He brings gifts
into our lives, much the same way that fruit appears in an
orchard—things like affection for others, exuberance about
life, serenity. We develop a willingness to stick with things, a
sense of compassion in the heart, and a conviction that a
basic holiness permeates things and people. We find ourselves
involved in loyal commitments, not needing to force our way
in life, able to marshal and direct our energies wisely.

—Galatians 5:22–23 MSG

Nn Oo Pp Qq Rr Ss Tt Uu Vv Ww Xx Yy Zz

TAKE TIME

Take time to work, it is the price of success.

Take time to think, it is the source of power.

Take time to play, it is the secret of perpetual youth.

Take time to read, it is the foundation of wisdom.

Take time to be friendly, it is the road to happiness.

Take time to dream, it is hitching your wagon to a star.

Take time to love and be loved, it is the privilege of the
gods,

Take time to look around, it is too short a day to be selfish.

Take time to laugh, it is the music of the soul.

—Old English Prayer

TEACHERS

Paint their minds
and guide their thoughts
Share their achievements
and advise their faults

Inspire a Love
Of knowledge and truth
As you light the path
Which leads our youth

For our future brightens
with each lesson you teach
Each smile you lengthen
Each goal you help reach

Nn Oo Pp Qq Rr Ss Tt Uu Vv Ww Xx Yy Zz

For the dawn of each poet

each philosopher and king

Begins with a Teacher

And the wisdom they bring

—Kevin William Huff

A TIME-TESTED PRAYER

Oh, that You would bless me indeed,
and enlarge my territory, that Your hand would
be with me, and that You would keep me
from evil, that I may not cause pain!

—The Prayer of Jabez, I Chronicles 4:10 NKJV

WORDS OF WISDOM

When inspiration does not come to me,
I go halfway to meet it.

—Sigmund Freud

Education is man's going forward from cocksure
ignorance to thoughtful uncertainty.

—Kenneth G. Johnson

Where there is an open mind,
there will always be a frontier.

—Charles F. Kettering

Vague and nebulous is the beginning
of all things, but not their end.

—Kahlil Gibran

A a B b C c D d E e F f G g H h I i J j K k L l M m

ALL THE ANSWERS

As a teacher, do you expect yourself to have all the answers? Is that even possible? But your students look to you as their resident expert. They think you are a fountain of knowledge, maybe even the smartest person on the planet—a good thing because you want their respect, but also a big responsibility. And sometimes they ask questions that have no answers.

"Why does Jamie's brother have cancer?"

"Why did Molly's daddy leave their family?"

"Can Grandpa hear me now that he's dead?"

"Why are so many African children sick?

Sometimes the best answer is to admit that you don't know everything and that there are some questions that have no answers. Sometimes the best response is to simply give a hug and then say, "I don't know, but I do care." Sometimes you simply need to repeat the question and listen to the child's answer, right or wrong. And then still give a hug. And sometimes you need to let them know that the only one with all the answers is God … and that we can take all our toughest questions to Him.

INQUISITIVE MINDS

Good teaching is more a giving of right questions
than a giving of right answers.

—Josef Albers

A helping word to one in trouble is often
like a switch on a railroad track ... an inch
between wreck and smooth, rolling prosperity.

—Henry Ward Beecher

He who is afraid to ask is ashamed of learning.

—Danish Proverb

Teachers open the door,
but you must enter by yourself.

—Chinese Proverb

To me the sole hope of human
salvation lies in teaching.

—George Bernard Shaw

Aa Bb Cc Dd Ee Ff Gg Hh Ii Jj Kk Ll Mm

BELIEVE

Believe in yourself,
In the power you have
To control your own life
Day by day.

Believe in the strength
That you have deep inside
And your faith will help
Show you the way.

Believe in tomorrow
And what it will bring.
Let a hopeful heart
Carry you through.

For things will work out
If you trust and believe.
There's no limit to
What you can do!

—Unknown

Nn Oo Pp Qq Rr Ss Tt Uu Vv Ww Xx Yy Zz

THE CREATION OF THE TEACHER

The Good Lord was creating teachers. It was His sixth day of "overtime," and He knew that this was a tremendous responsibility, for teachers would touch the lives of so many impressionable young children.

An angel appeared to Him and said, "You are taking a long time to figure this one out."

"Yes," said the Lord, "but have you read the specs on this order?"

Teacher:

- must stand above all students, yet be on their level
- must be able to do 180 things not connected with the subject being taught
- must run on coffee and leftovers
- must communicate vital knowledge to all students daily and be right most of the time
- must have more time for others than for herself/himself
- must have a smile that can endure through pay cuts, problematic children, and worried parents
- must have six pairs of hands

- must go on teaching when parents question every move and others are not supportive

"Six pair of hands," said the angel. "That's impossible."

"Well," said the Lord, "it isn't the hands that are the problem. It's the three pairs of eyes that are presenting the most difficulty!"

The angel looked incredulous and asked, "Three pairs of eyes … on a standard model?"

The Lord nodded His head. "One pair can see a student for what he is and not what others have labeled him as. Another pair of eyes is in the back of the teacher's head to see what should not be seen, but what must be known. The eyes in the front are only to look at the child as he/she 'acts out' in order to reflect, 'I understand and I still believe in you,' without so much as saying a word to the child."

"Lord," said the angel, "this is a very large project and I think you should work on it tomorrow."

"I can't," said the Lord, "for I have come very close to creating something much like myself. I have one that comes to work when he/she is sick … teaches a class of children that do not want to learn … has a special place in his/her heart for children who are not his/her own … understands the struggles of those who have difficulty … never takes the students for granted…."

Nn Oo Pp Qq Rr Ss Tt Uu Vv Ww Xx Yy Zz

The angel looked closely at the model the Lord was creating. "It is too soft-hearted," said the angel.

"Yes," said the Lord, "but also tough. You cannot imagine what this teacher can endure or do, if necessary."

"Can this teacher think?" asked the angel.

"Not only think," said the Lord, "but reason and compromise."

The angel came closer to have a better look at the model and ran his finger over the teacher's cheek. "Well, Lord," said the angel, "your job looks fine but there is a leak. I told you that you were putting too much into this model. You cannot imagine the stress that will be placed upon the teacher."

The Lord moved in closer and lifted the drop of moisture from the teacher's cheek. It shone and glistened in the light. "It is not a leak," He said. "It's a tear."

"A tear? What is that?" asked the angel. "What is a tear for?"

The Lord replied with great thought, "It is for the joy and pride of seeing a child accomplish even the smallest task. It is for the loneliness of children who have a hard time fitting in, and it is for compassion for the feelings of their parents. It comes from the pain of not being able to reach some children and the disappointment those children feel in themselves. It comes often when a teacher has been with a class for a year and must say good-bye to those students and get ready to welcome a new class."

"My," said the angel, "the tear thing is a great idea. You're a genius!"

The Lord looked somber and replied, "I didn't put it there."

—Unknown

NOT FOR THE MONEY

A gifted teacher is as rare as a gifted doctor, and makes far less money.

—Unknown

Good teachers are costly, but bad teachers cost more.

—Bob Talbert

Teaching is leaving a vestige of oneself in the development of another. And surely the student is a bank where you can deposit your most precious treasures.

—Eugene P. Bertin

Work like you don't need the money.

—Unknown

Aa Bb Cc Dd Ee Ff Gg Hh Ii Jj Kk Ll Mm

THE RIPPLING EFFECT

Drop a stone into the water—

In a moment it is gone.

But there are a hundred ripples

Circling on and on and on—

Say a word of cheer and splendor—

In a moment it is gone

But there are a hundred ripples

Circling on and on.

—Unknown

POWER OF
THE POSITIVE

You have to expect things of yourself
before you can do them.

—Michael Jordan

Ability is what you're capable of doing.
Motivation determines what you do.
Attitude determines how well you do it.

—Lou Holtz

Whether you believe you can do
a thing or not, you are right.

—Henry Ford

You are educated when you have the ability
to listen to almost anything without
losing your temper or self-confidence.

—Robert Frost

Aa Bb Cc Dd Ee Ff Gg Hh Ii Jj Kk Ll Mm

HAND IN HAND
WITH GOD

When God is our companion

As we walk the road of life,

There is help for every problem,

And grace for care and strife,

And we'll find that we've been happy

All along the path we've trod,

When, in faith, we've made the journey,

Hand in hand along with God.

—Unknown

BRIGHT BEGINNINGS

Be faithful in small things because it is
in them that your strength lies.

—Mother Teresa

Train up a child in the way he should go,
and when he is old he will not depart from it.

—Proverbs 22:6 NKJV

THE HAND HOLDERS

There is no job more important than yours,

No job anywhere else in the land.

You are the keepers of the future;

You hold the smallest of hands.

Into your care you are trusted

To nurture and care for the young,

And for all of your everyday heroics,

Your talents and skills go unsung.

You wipe tears from the eyes of the injured.

You rock babies brand-new in your arms.

You encourage the shy and unsure child.

You make sure they are safe from all harm.

You foster the bonds of friendships,

Letting no child go away mad.

Nn Oo Pp Qq Rr Ss Tt Uu Vv Ww Xx Yy Zz

You respect and you honor their emotions.

You give hugs to each child when they're sad.

You have more impact than does a professor,

A child's mind is molded by four;

So whatever you lay on the table

Is whatever the child will explore.

Give each child the tools for adventure,

Let them be artists and writers and more;

Let them fly on the wind and dance on the stars

And build castles of sand on the shore.

It is true that you don't make much money

And you don't get a whole lot of praise,

But when one small child says, "I love you,"

You're reminded of how this job pays.

—Dori Rossmann

MORE TIMELESS TIDBITS

Teaching should be full of ideas,

not stuffed with facts.

—Unknown

A teacher affects eternity; he can never tell

where his influence stops.

—Henry Adams

Education is not filling a bucket, but lighting a fire.

—William Butler Yeats

You can teach a lesson for a day, but if you

teach curiosity, you teach for a lifetime.

—Unknown

Cc Dd Ee Ff Gg Hh Ii Jj Kk Ll Mm Nn Oo Pp Qq Rr Ss Tt Uu Vv Ww Xx Yy

Spring Blossoms

Those little seeds of learning have germinated
Warmed by the sunlight of knowledge
Watered by wise words of instruction
Nurtured by loving acts of kindness
Strong young minds, like eager seedling evergreens
Now stretch eagerly toward
The light of understanding
Growing strong and tall and sturdy
And able to stand on their own.

REMEMBER THE
CHILD WITHIN

How can we expect to truly reach children, transform fresh minds, touch young hearts, inspire real learning, if we can't remember what it was like to be a child—if we have become so caught up in our "grown-up" responsibilities that we lose touch with that little girl or boy who is tucked somewhere deep within us? Unless we can relate to childhood, we cannot expect to connect with real children.

Can you remember dour-faced teachers who seemed older than Methuselah—the kind who'd always watch for a kid to blow it? One mistake, and they'd let 'em have it—and good. Can you recall anything childlike about one of those teachers? Anything that connected with your own youth, spontaneity, and free spirit? Probably not. Most likely those are not the types of teachers who inspired you to teach, unless it was to convince you that you could do it better.

Somehow it seems easy to get caught up in the adult world and forget what it's like to be a child. Easy to forget that we don't really have all the answers. Easy to neglect to ask those fresh and challenging questions. Easy to not try new things or welcome different experiences. Easy to stifle curiosity by choosing to stick with the tried and true. Easy to play it safe.

Before you know it, you could easily become old and stuffy, just like those teachers you never liked. Worst of all, you could lose that sweet, simple joy of everyday living.

If this has happened to you, remember that it's never too late. Unlike many of your adult peers (who work around grown-ups all day), you have a built-in "anti-aging" protective barrier. Take a good, long look at those little lives all around you. Study them and remember what it's like to be young. Soon you will be able to welcome your own "child" back to the surface. Once again, you will laugh and play and celebrate the freshness of life!

What a blessing it is to be linked, hand in hand, with children!

YOU WERE THERE

When I needed encouragement, you gave me a pep talk

When I required help, you rolled up your sleeves

When I wanted to talk, you were ready to listen

When I needed a hug, you opened your arms

When I had to vent, you lent me your ears

When I needed a nudge, you gave me an elbow

When I required correction, you did it ever so gently

When I all I could do was cry, you cried right along
    with me

And when I needed to pray, you opened your heart

A a B b C c D d E e F f G g H h I i J j K k L l M m

HOW TO STAY FOREVER YOUNG

Youth is not a time of life, it is a state of mind.

You are as old as your doubt, your fear, your despair.

The way to keep young is to keep your faith young.

Keep your self-confidence young.

Keep your hope young.

—Luella F. Phean

But those who wait on the LORD shall renew
their strength; they shall mount up with wings
like eagles, they shall run and not be weary,
they shall walk and not faint.

—Isaiah 40:31 NKJV

HOW DO YOU SPELL
TEACHER?

T is for tolerance, thoughtfulness, and tenderness—to show the gentle way.

E is for enthusiasm, excitement, and energy—to brighten up the day.

A is for aptitude, ability, and action—the skills to see you through.

C is for caring, comfort, and charity—in all you say and do.

H is for helpful, happy, and handy—with these you can't go wrong.

E is for equity, empathy, and encouragement—to help kids get along.

R is for resourceful, responsible, and reasonable—you just can't get enough.

So, that's how you spell teacher—one who's made of the right stuff!

A a B b C c D d E e F f G g H h I i J j K k L l M m

CHARACTER BUILDING

Our character is what we do
when we think no one is looking.

—H. Jackson Brown Jr.

Promise yourself to be so strong that nothing
can disturb your peace of mind.

—Christian D. Larson

Our deeds determine us, as much as
we determine our deeds.

—George Eliot

People grow through experience if they
meet life honestly and courageously.
This is how character is built.

—Eleanor Roosevelt

TIME FOR ALL THINGS

For everything there is a season, and a time for every matter under heaven: a time to be born, and a time to die; a time to plant, and a time to pluck up what is planted; a time to kill, and a time to heal; a time to break down, and a time to build up; a time to weep, and a time to laugh; a time to mourn, and a time to dance; a time to throw away stones, and a time to gather stones together; a time to embrace, and a time to refrain from embracing; a time to seek, and a time to lose; a time to keep, and a time to throw away; a time to tear, and a time to sew; a time to keep silence, and a time to speak; a time to love, and a time to hate; a time for war, and a time for peace.

—Ecclesiastes 3:1–8 NRSV

A a   B b   C c   D d   E e   F f   G g   H h   I i   J j   K k   L l   M m

HUGS

It's wondrous what a hug can do.

A hug can cheer you when you're blue.

A hug can say, "I love you so!"

Or "Gee, I hate to see you go."

A hug can soothe a small child's pain

And bring a rainbow after rain.

The HUG—there's just no doubt about it—

We scarcely could survive without it.

Hugs are great for fathers and mothers,

Sweet for sisters, as well as brothers.

Chances are some favorite aunt

Loves them more than potted plants.

Kittens crave them,

Puppies love them,

Heads of state

Are not above them.

A hug can break the language barrier,

And make the dullest day seem merrier.

No need to fret about the store of 'em.

The more you give, there's only more of 'em.

So stretch those arms without delay,

And give someone a hug today!

—Unknown

A a   B b   C c   D d   E e   F f   G g   H h   I i   J j   K k   L l   M m

IN MY LIFETIME

In my lifetime

I hope to develop

Arms that are strong

Hands that are gentle

Ears that will listen

Eyes that are kind

A mind full of wisdom

A heart that understands

A tongue that will speak softly.

—Unknown

WHOLEHEARTEDLY

If you have zest and enthusiasm you attract
zest and enthusiasm. Life does give back in kind.

—Norman Vincent Peale

It's always the challenge of the future,
this feeling of excitement, that drives me.

—Yoshihisa Tabuchi

Like what you do.

—Paul Harvey

Life's blows cannot break a person whose spirit
is warmed at the fire of enthusiasm.

—Norman Vincent Peale

A a B b C c D d E e F f G g H h I i J j K k L l M m

LOVE FINDS A WAY

I am done with great things and big plans, great institutions
and big success. I am for those tiny, invisible, loving human
forces that work from individual to individual, creeping
through the crannies of the world like so many rootlets, or
like the capillary oozing of water, which, if given time, will
rend the hardest monuments of pride.

—William James

TEACHABLE MOMENTS

Sometimes you have a perfect plan
For how the day should start,
But despite all your efforts
The whole thing falls apart.

Perhaps it is a missing link
Or something very small,
But soon you know your lesson planned
Will never work at all!

But think about the ruined plans
Of a flustered miner of old;
He never saw a speck of tin—
Instead, he found real gold!

So take a breath and look around,
Then say a silent prayer,
And perhaps you'll find the answer tucked
Within the problem there.

VISIONARIES

There is more to us than we know.
If we can be made to see it, perhaps for the rest of
our lives we will be unwilling to settle for less.

—Kurt Hahn

To accomplish great things we must first dream,
then visualize, then plan ... believe ... act!

—Alfred A. Montapert

The process of learning requires not only
hearing and applying but also forgetting
and then remembering again.

—John Gray

Vision is the ability to see God's presence,
plan, and power over obstacles.

—Mike Breaux

Nn Oo Pp Qq Rr Ss Tt Uu Vv Ww Xx Yy Zz

WHEN YOU THOUGHT
I WASN'T LOOKING

When you thought I wasn't looking

You hung my first painting on the refrigerator

And I wanted to paint another.

When you thought I wasn't looking

You fed a stray cat

And I thought it was good to be kind to animals.

When you thought I wasn't looking

You baked a birthday cake just for me

And I knew that little things were special things.

When you thought I wasn't looking

You said a prayer

And I believed there was a God that I could always talk to.

When you thought I wasn't looking

You kissed me good-night

And I felt loved.

When you thought I wasn't looking
I saw tears come from your eyes
And I learned that sometimes things hurt—
But that it's alright to cry.

When you thought I wasn't looking
You smiled
And it made me want to look that pretty too.

When you thought I wasn't looking
You cared
And I wanted to be everything I could be.

When you thought I wasn't looking—
I looked …
And wanted to say thanks
For all those things you did
When you thought I wasn't looking.

—Mary Rita Schilke Korzan

"RANDOM" ACTS OF KINDNESS

In years to come a child may forget
what you taught him, but he will always remember
how you made him feel.

—Unknown

Our job is not to straighten each other out,
but to help each other up.

—Neva Cole

The secret of education lies in respecting the pupil.

—Ralph Waldo Emerson

People don't care how much you know
until they know how much you care!

—Unknown

A a B b C c D d E e F f G g H h I i J j K k L l M m

There is never enough time to do or say all the things that we would wish; the thing is to do as much as you can in the time that you have.

—Charles Dickens

LEAVE SOMETHING BEHIND

Spread love everywhere you go:

First of all, in your own house,

Give love to your children,

To your wife or husband,

To a next door neighbor....

Let no one ever come to you

Without leaving better or happier.

Be the living expression of God's kindness;

Kindness in your face,

Kindness in your eyes,

Kindness in your smile,

Kindness in your warm greeting.

—Mother Teresa

SEIZE THE DAY!

The grass is green, the birds are singing,
With bees and flowers and butterflies out.
But inside the school, it's hot and muggy,
With kids distracted and prowling about.

Perhaps it's time to get creative,
To open the windows of your mind,
And take the science project outdoors,
To look and see what you can find!

For each day has some wisdom in it,
Something new to celebrate!
But be aware, or you might miss it,
Stuck inside, one day too late.

For we don't know what comes tomorrow—
Rainy skies or aptitude tests?
So, let's learn to seize the moment,
For life lessons are the best!

TEACHING TIDBITS

Even a happy life cannot be without a
measure of darkness, and the word *happy* would
lose its meaning if it were not balanced by sadness.
It is far better to take things as they come along
with patience and equanimity.

—Carl Jung

The art of teaching is the art of assisting discovery.

—Mark Van Doren

The important thing is not so much that
every child should be taught, as that every child
should be given the wish to learn.

—John Lubbock

No one can become really educated without having
pursued some study in which he took no interest.

—T. S. Eliot

Aa Bb Cc Dd Ee Ff Gg Hh Ii Jj Kk Ll Mm

NO REGRETS

As the school year winds down (or up, depending on your perspective), do you begin to wonder, Did I do enough? Did I reach out enough? Did Jenny make enough progress? Did Johnny learn to read well enough? Did I really connect with my class? Will they remember this year with fondness? Should I have done something differently?

All of these doubts, though troubling, only show how much you care—and caring is always where good education begins. And, honestly, how is it possible to really measure your effectiveness as a teacher? CAT scores? Teacher evaluations? Test scores can be skewed, and children can act up while their teacher is being observed. So, how will you know if your year was a true success?

Perhaps there's no sure way to be absolutely certain of how we rate as teachers, so maybe it would be best to learn to tune into that quiet, small voice that whispers words of sweet assurance somewhere deep inside of us. The voice that might be saying, "Well done, good servant." Or perhaps we need to embrace a bit of faith and believe that if we did our very best, then someday, somehow, good will spring forth from it.

In truth, the best way to know if we've succeeded is to look at the faces of those who have been in our care. Children aren't usually that good at hiding their feelings, so if those faces are happy and smiling and ignited, then chances are we've done a great job. So let's have no regrets. We must remember that we're still learning too, and there's always next year to become even better!

RESPECT

We confide in our strength, without boasting of it;
we respect that of others, without fearing it.

—Thomas Jefferson

Respect for ourselves guides our morals;
respect for others guides our manners.

—Laurence Sterne

There are admirable potentialities in every human
being. Believe in your strength and your youth.
Learn to repeat endlessly to yourself,
"It all depends on me."

—André Gide

Respect commands itself and it can neither
be given nor withheld when it is due.

—Eldridge Cleaver

Nn Oo Pp Qq Rr Ss Tt Uu Vv Ww Xx Yy Zz

IT TAKES JUST ONE

One song can spark a moment,
One flower can wake the dream.
One tree can start a forest,
One bird can herald the spring.

One smile begins a friendship,
One handclasp lifts a soul.
One star can guide a ship at sea,
One word can frame the goal.

One vote can change a nation,
One sunbeam lights a room.
One candle wipes out darkness,
One laugh will conquer gloom.

One step must start each journey,

One word must start each prayer.

One hope will raise our spirits,

One touch can show you care.

One voice can speak with wisdom,

One heart can know what's true.

One life can make the difference,

You see, it's up to YOU!

—Unknown

PERSEVERING

If your plan is for one year, plant rice.

If your plan is for ten years, plant trees.

If your plan is for a hundred years, educate children.

—Confucius

Only if you reach the boundary will the boundary recede before you. And if you don't, if you confine your efforts, the boundary will shrink to accommodate itself to your efforts. And you can only expand your capacities by working to the very limit.

—Hugh Nibley

Champions keep playing until they get it right.

—Billie Jean King

To teach is to touch a life forever.

—Unknown

Aa Bb Cc Dd Ee Ff Gg Hh Ii Jj Kk Ll Mm

UNITY

I dreamed I stood in a studio
And watched two sculptors there.
The clay they used was a young child's mind,
And they fashioned it with care.

One was a teacher—the tools she used
Were books, music, and art.
The other, a parent—working with a guiding hand,
And a gentle, loving heart.

Day after day, the teacher toiled
With a touch that was careful, deft, and sure,
While the parent labored by her side
And polished and smoothed it o'er.

And when at last, their task was done
They were proud of what they had wrought,

For the things they had molded into the child
Could neither be sold nor bought.

And each agree they would have failed
If each had worked alone,
For behind the parent stood the school,
And behind the teacher, the home.

—Ray A. Lingenfelter

TRUE TEACHING

To teach is to learn again!

—Oliver Wendell Holmes

A teacher is one who makes himself
progressively unnecessary.

—Thomas Carruthers

No matter how good teaching may be, each student
must take the responsibility for his own education.

—John Carolus, SJ

The true teacher defends his pupils against
his own personal influence.

—Amos Bronson Alcott

Nn Oo Pp Qq Rr Ss Tt Uu Vv Ww Xx Yy Zz

TO THINK UPON

In a completely rational society, the best of us
would aspire to be teachers and the rest would
have to settle for something less, because passing
civilization along from one generation to the next
ought to be the highest honor and highest
responsibility anyone could have.

—Lee Iacocca

The mediocre teacher tells.
The good teacher explains.
The superior teacher demonstrates.
The great teacher inspires.

—William Arthur Ward

There are no hands so small that they
cannot make a difference in the world.

—Unknown

A a B b C c D d E e F f G g H h I i J j K k L l M m

A DAY WELL SPENT

If you sit down at set of sun

And count the acts that you have done,

And, counting, find

One self-denying deed, one word

That eased the heart of him who heard—

One glance most kind,

That fell like sunshine where it went—

Then you may count that day well spent.

—George Eliot

SLOW DANCE

Have you ever watched kids on a merry-go-round,

Or listened to rain slapping the ground?

Ever followed a butterfly's erratic flight,

Or gazed at the sun as it fades into night?

You'd better slow down, don't dance so fast,

Time is short, the music won't last.

Do you run through each day on the fly?

When you ask, "How are you?" do you hear the reply?

When the day is done, do you lie in your bed,

With the next hundred chores running through your head?

You'd better slow down, don't dance so fast.

Time is short, the music won't last.

Ever told your child, "We'll do it tomorrow,"

And in your haste, not see his sorrow?

Ever lost touch, let a good friendship die,

A a B b C c D d E e F f G g H h I i J j K k L l M m

'Cause you never had time to call and say, "Hi"?

You'd better slow down, don't dance so fast.

Time is short, the music won't last.

When you run so fast to get somewhere,

You miss half the fun of getting there.

When you worry and hurry through your day,

It's like an unopened gift ... thrown away.

Life is not a race. Do take it slower.

Hear the music before the song is over.

—David L. Weatherford

BREAKTHROUGH

My heart is singing for joy this morning.
A miracle has happened! The light of understanding
has shone upon my little pupil's mind,
and behold, all things are changed.

—Anne Sullivan

A PARENT'S THANKS

What's nearer and dearer to a parent's heart

Than a beloved child, so sweet and so smart?

A child that's entrusted over to you,

To lead and to guide the whole year through.

And all that you teach and instruct him to be—

The way that you touch him is how you touch me.

For he is my treasure (sent from God up above)

To nurture and cherish, to discipline in love.

So how can I thank you for how you've cared,

Molding and shaping this child we have shared?

Mere words can't describe all I'd like to say—

May God bless you and keep you along your way!

A TEACHER FOR
ALL SEASONS

A teacher is like Spring,

Who nurtures new green sprouts,

Encourages and leads them,

Whenever they have doubts.

A teacher is like Summer,

Whose sunny temperament

Makes studying a pleasure,

Preventing discontent.

A teacher is like Fall,

With methods crisp and clear,

Lessons of bright colors

And a happy atmosphere.

A a   B b   C c   D d   E e   F f   G g   H h   I i   J j   K k   L l   M m

A teacher is like Winter,
While it's snowing hard outside,
Keeping students comfortable,
As a warm and helpful guide.

Teacher, you do all these things,
With a pleasant attitude;
You're a teacher for all seasons,
And you have my gratitude!

—Joanna Fuchs

FINAL THOUGHTS

Better to do something imperfectly
than to do nothing flawlessly.

—Robert Schuller

Mistakes are the portals of discovery.

—James Joyce

Difficulties are meant to rouse, not discourage.
The human spirit is to grow strong by conflict.

—William Ellery Channing

To teach well, we need not say all that we know,
only what is useful for the pupil to hear.

—Unknown

Aa Bb Cc Dd Ee Ff Gg Hh Ii Jj Kk Ll Mm

PROMISES

Better than a thousand days of diligent study

is one day with a great teacher.

—Japanese Proverb

A good teacher is like a candle—

it consumes itself to light the way for others.

—Unknown

Nn Oo Pp Qq Rr Ss Tt Uu Vv Ww Xx Yy Zz

THANK YOU FOR BEING MY TEACHER!

Thank you for all that you've done for me

Since I stepped in your classroom last fall.

You gave me so much, day after day,

Your patience, your humor, your all!

Thank you for treating me with respect

And showing me when I was wrong.

Thank you for helping in so many ways,

You encouraged me all the year long!

Thank you!

HONOR BOOKS
expressions of faith, hope, and love

It was he who gave some to be ... teachers, to prepare God's people for works of service, so that the body of Christ may be built up until we all reach unity in the faith and in the knowledge of the Son of God and become mature, attaining to the whole measure of the fullness of Christ.
EPHESIANS 4:11–13

_____

Anyone who breaks one of the least of these commandments and teaches others to do the same will be called least in the kingdom of heaven, but whoever practices and teaches these commands will be called great in the kingdom of heaven.
MATTHEW 5:19

_____

Command and teach these things. Don't let anyone look down on you because you are young, but set an example for the believers in speech, in life, in love, in faith and in purity.
1 TIMOTHY 4:11–12

Lord, I know that you have led me to this position, to this role of being a teacher. But so often I feel unworthy of the responsibility I have to shape these young minds. Give me the ability to create a stable and fun environment of learning in my classroom. I ask for your wisdom as I teach. Give me the ability to effectively reach each child in my classroom and help me to recognize when they are struggling. Father, I need the grace to communicate your divine love to each child who enters my classroom. Amen.

BUT THE GREATEST OF THESE IS LOVE!

If I speak with human eloquence and angelic ecstasy but don't love, I'm nothing but the creaking of a rusty gate. If I speak God's Word with power, revealing all his mysteries and making everything plain as day, and if I have faith that says to a mountain, "Jump," and it jumps, but I don't love, I'm nothing. If I give everything I own to the poor and even go to the stake to be burned as a martyr, but I don't love, I've gotten nowhere. So, no matter what I say, what I believe, and what I do, I'm bankrupt without love. Love never gives up. Love cares more for others than for self. Love doesn't want what it doesn't have. Love doesn't strut, doesn't have a swelled head, doesn't force itself on others, isn't always "me first," doesn't fly off the handle, doesn't keep score of the sins of others, doesn't revel when others grovel, takes pleasure in the flowering of truth, puts up with anything, trusts God always, always looks for the best, never looks back, but keeps going to the end. Love never dies. Inspired speech will be over some day; praying in tongues will end; understanding will reach its limit. We know only a portion of the truth, and what we say about God is always incomplete. But when the Complete arrives, our incompletes will be canceled. When I was an infant at my mother's breast, I gurgled and cooed like any infant. When I grew up, I left those infant ways for good. We don't yet see things clearly. We're squinting in a fog, peering through a mist. But it won't be long before the weather clears and the sun shines bright! We'll see it all then, see it all as clearly as God sees us, knowing him directly just as he knows us! *But for right now, until that completeness, we have three things to do to lead us toward that consummation: Trust steadily in God, hope unswervingly, love extravagantly. And the best of the three is love* (1 Cor. 13:1–13).